Contents

Who Is
Michelle Obama?

by Megan Stine

illustrated by John O'Brien

Penguin Workshop
An Imprint of Penguin Random House

For Jane O'Connor, with gratitude and admiration—MS

For my sister Joanne—JOB

PENGUIN WORKSHOP
Penguin Young Readers Group
An Imprint of Penguin Random House LLC

Text copyright © 2013 by Megan Stine. Illustrations copyright © 2013 by John O'Brien. Cover illustration copyright © 2013 by Penguin Random House LLC. All rights reserved. Published by Penguin Workshop, an imprint of Penguin Random House LLC, 345 Hudson Street, New York, New York 10014. PENGUIN and PENGUIN WORKSHOP are trademarks of Penguin Books Ltd. WHO HQ & Design is a registered trademark of Penguin Random House LLC. Printed in the USA.

Library of Congress Control Number: 2013017264

ISBN 9780448478630

28 27 26 25

Who Is
Michelle Obama?

A tall and beautiful African American woman stood on the lawn behind the White House. She smiled at a group of children and teenagers who had come from nearby schools.

It was a warm sunny day in October. The kids were dressed in T-shirts and jeans. The woman wore a bright blue sweater and black slacks. Grinning, she picked up a hula hoop and began to swivel it around her waist.

The crowd watched, and someone started counting. "Ninety-eight . . . ninety-nine . . . one hundred . . . one hundred one . . ."

She kept going. She reached 142 times before she stopped. She could have kept going longer!

"I can hula-hoop forever," the woman said. She

even knew how to swirl two hoops at once.

The kids tried to keep up with her. Everybody was having fun. But there was also an important purpose to the fun. Hula-hooping was a way to help kids get more exercise and stay healthy.

Who was that gorgeous woman performing at the White House? It was Michelle Obama, the First Lady of the United States!

HILLARY CLINTON
OCTOBER 26, 1947–

WHEN BILL CLINTON RAN FOR PRESIDENT IN 1992, HE TOLD VOTERS THAT THEY WOULD GET "TWO FOR THE PRICE OF ONE." HE MEANT THAT HE AND HILLARY WOULD WORK TOGETHER ONCE THEY WERE IN THE WHITE HOUSE.

SOME PEOPLE DIDN'T LIKE THAT IDEA. HILLARY, HOWEVER, WAS SMART AND EAGER TO DO GOOD WORK. SHE WOULDN'T LET ANYTHING STAND IN HER WAY.

SHE WAS THE FIRST FIRST LADY TO HAVE HER OWN OFFICE IN THE WEST WING OF THE WHITE HOUSE, NEAR THE PRESIDENT'S. OTHER FIRST LADIES HAD THEIR OFFICES IN THE EAST WING— OUT OF THE WAY.

SHE WAS THE FIRST FIRST LADY TO WORK DIRECTLY WITH CONGRESS TO TRY TO GET A NEW HEALTH CARE LAW PASSED. CONGRESS REJECTED HER IDEAS, THOUGH.

AFTER BILL CLINTON WAS NO LONGER PRESIDENT, SHE DECIDED TO RUN FOR OFFICE HERSELF. SHE WAS THE FIRST FIRST LADY TO DO THAT! IN 2000, SHE WAS ELECTED AS US SENATOR—THE FIRST *WOMAN* TO SERVE AS A SENATOR FROM NEW YORK.

IN 2008, SHE RAN FOR PRESIDENT AGAINST BARACK OBAMA. SHE DIDN'T GET THE NOMINATION. BUT AFTER BARACK OBAMA WAS ELECTED, HE APPOINTED HILLARY CLINTON AS SECRETARY OF STATE. THAT MADE HER THE FIRST FORMER FIRST LADY TO SERVE IN A CABINET POST.

Chapter 1
A Close Family

7436 SOUTH EUCLID AVENUE

Michelle LaVaughn Robinson was born on
January 17, 1964, on the South Side of Chicago.
Her family lived in a one-bedroom apartment.
It was on the second floor of a small house.
Michelle's great-aunt lived downstairs.

Michelle's parents slept in one room. They divided the other room. One space was a tiny bedroom for Craig, Michelle's brother. He was two years older than Michelle. The other space was a tiny bedroom for Michelle. It was as small as a closet!

Michelle's parents were strict, but she didn't mind. How could she, when she admired them so much?

Her father, Fraser Robinson, was a hard worker and a cheerful man. For years, he held a job with the city water plant. He worked his way up from janitor to manager. Fraser's job was tough. It got even harder after he became sick. When Michelle was young, he developed a disease called multiple sclerosis. It affected his spine and muscles. It was hard for him to walk. He had to use crutches or a cane. Sometimes it took Fraser Robinson an hour to get dressed. Still, Fraser never complained. He never skipped work because he didn't feel well.

Michelle and Craig never wanted to disappoint their father. If one of them ever misbehaved, Fraser would give them a stare. Then he would say, "I'm disappointed." That's all it took. Michelle and Craig would *both* start crying—even if only *one* of them had done something wrong!

Michelle also looked up to her mother, Marian Robinson. She had been a secretary, but when her children were born, she quit work to stay home

Chicago

with them. Like Fraser, she expected a lot from
her children—good grades, good behavior. She
brought home extra workbooks so Michelle could
study more in her spare time.

Marian also taught Michelle and Craig to speak their own minds and stand up for themselves. "Make sure you respect your teachers," Marian Robinson said. "But don't hesitate to question them."

Life at home was simple and happy. The family always ate dinner together.

At night, they played board games such as
Monopoly and chess. Michelle always wanted to
win. Craig had to *let* her win sometimes or else
she'd quit. Then he wouldn't have anyone to play
with!

Michelle and Craig were allowed only an hour
of television each night. They had pizza only once
or twice a year! But they always felt cherished and

loved, and knew their parents believed they were capable of anything.

On Sunday nights, the family visited Michelle's grandparents, who lived nearby. But when Michelle was ten, her grandparents moved back to South Carolina. Her grandfather had grown up there.

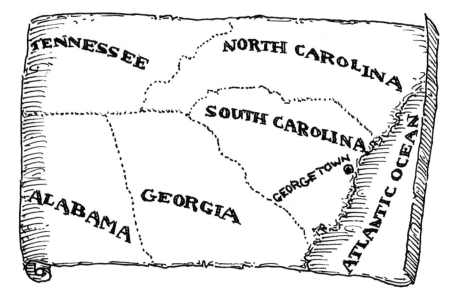

After that, Michelle and her family drove to South Carolina each summer. Many of Michelle's

aunts, uncles, and cousins also lived there. Her
visits were fun and carefree.

Michelle didn't know then that her family—
and South Carolina—had a dark past. Slavery.

Michelle's great-great-grandfather had been a
slave in South Carolina. He lived in an area called
Georgetown. Georgetown was part of the "low
country" of South Carolina. It was wet, soggy
land near the ocean—perfect for growing rice.
But growing rice was very hard work. It took
more slaves to plant and harvest rice than any
other crop.

Michelle Obama's great-great-grandfather was named Jim Robinson. He worked on a plantation called Friendfield. At one time, Friendfield had as many as five hundred slaves. The plantation owner's family lived in a big, fancy white house. Jim Robinson lived in a small slave cabin on a street called Slave Street.

Jim Robinson never learned to read or write, not even when he became a free man after the Civil War ended. But his second son, Fraser—Michelle's great-grandfather—learned how. Fraser worked doing house chores for a white family named Nesmith. The Nesmiths had several young daughters. Fraser saw how important learning was in the Nesmith house. He watched as the Nesmiths pushed their daughters to do well in school.

Pretty soon, Fraser decided that he wanted to learn how to read, too. He was so determined, his relatives say he taught himself!

From early on, the Robinson family always valued education. Fraser Sr. taught his son to study hard and learn as much as possible. In turn, Fraser Jr. taught Michelle's father, Fraser III, the same thing.

Michelle didn't know any of this family history when she visited Georgetown as a child. All she knew was that she was surrounded by people who believed in hard work and education. That's what it took to succeed and have a good life.

Chapter 2
Making the Grades

It was a Robinson family tradition to skip second grade. Both of Michelle's parents had skipped second grade. So had her brother Craig.

Michelle worked as hard as they had. So she skipped second grade, too!

At Bryn Mawr Public Elementary School, Michelle got all As. But one teacher complained about Michelle to her mother. She said Michelle had a temper. Her mother just laughed. "Yeah, she's got a temper," Marian Robinson said. "But we decided to keep her anyway!"

When Michelle reached sixth grade, she was chosen for a gifted program. It meant she could take some classes at a nearby college! She studied biology—she even learned how to dissect a rat.

She also started learning French that year.

After school, Michelle took piano lessons from her great-aunt who lived downstairs. She practiced her piano lessons without ever being reminded. Her mother said, "She would practice the piano for so long, you would have to tell her to stop!"

MARTHA WASHINGTON
JUNE 2, 1731–MAY 22, 1802

MARTHA DANDRIDGE WAS A RICH YOUNG WIDOW WITH TWO CHILDREN WHEN SHE MARRIED GEORGE WASHINGTON IN 1759.

MARTHA LOVED GEORGE SO MUCH THAT SHE FOLLOWED HIM EVERYWHERE. WHEN HE WAS A GENERAL LEADING TROOPS IN THE REVOLUTIONARY WAR, MARTHA WENT WITH HIM. SHE EVEN FOLLOWED HIM TO COLD WINTER CAMPSITES COVERED IN SNOW.

WHEN THE WAR WAS OVER, GEORGE WASHINGTON WAS A HERO. EVERYONE WANTED HIM TO BE THE FIRST PRESIDENT OF THE UNITED STATES.

EVERYONE EXCEPT MARTHA, THAT IS. SHE DIDN'T WANT HIM TO BE ELECTED, AND SHE REFUSED TO ATTEND HIS INAUGURATION. BUT ONCE HE WAS ELECTED, SHE TOOK ON THE DUTIES OF FIRST LADY.

NO ONE USED THE TERM "FIRST LADY" IN THOSE DAYS, THOUGH. THEY CALLED HER LADY WASHINGTON OR "THE LADY PRESIDENTESS."

When Michelle graduated from Bryn Mawr Public Elementary, she was a top student. She wondered: Should she go to the nearby high school? Or was there a better choice?

Michelle and her parents talked it over. A new magnet school had opened in Chicago. A magnet school pulls in good students from all over a city. The school was called Whitney M. Young Magnet High School.

WHITNEY M. YOUNG MAGNET HIGH SCHOOL

It was one of the first in Chicago that tried for an even mix of black and white students. The only problem was that the school was twelve miles away from the Robinsons' house. It took an hour and a half to get there. Michelle would have to take two city buses, all by herself!

It was the best school, so Michelle decided to go.

For the next four years, Michelle worked hard. Taking tests sometimes gave her trouble. But that just made Michelle study harder the next time. She got all As, and still had time to take dance lessons. She was treasurer of the student council. She was in the National Honor Society—a club for excellent students.

One of Michelle's friends in high school was Santita Jackson, the daughter of Reverend Jesse Jackson. Jesse Jackson was a famous civil rights leader. He had worked with Martin Luther King Jr. In 1988, he had tried to become the first black Democratic candidate for president.

Of course the big question in high school was: What about college? Again, Michelle wanted the best. Her brother, Craig, was already enrolled at Princeton. Michelle wanted to go there, too.

But Craig was different from Michelle. He was a basketball star. He was also a great student who hardly had to study. Michelle's mother said that Craig could "pass a test just by carrying a book under his arm." When Michelle talked about going to Princeton, the counselor at the high school said no. Her test scores weren't high enough. She hadn't played sports.

Michelle never took no for an answer, though. She thought about Craig and his study habits, and she thought to herself, "I can do that, too." So she applied and was accepted.

In the fall of 1981, Michelle arrived at the beautiful campus in Princeton, New Jersey. The college was more than two hundred years old. Many of the stone buildings were covered in ivy. Huge leafy trees lined all the walkways. The dorms were charming old buildings with cozy rooms. The dining halls were incredible huge rooms with long tables, arched ceilings, and giant old chandeliers. They looked like scenes from a Harry Potter movie!

Right away Michelle noticed that there weren't many black people at Princeton. In Chicago, her neighborhood had been almost totally black. Her high school had been about half black.

At Princeton, most of the students were white—and a lot of them were rich. They drove expensive cars—BMWs! She didn't even know *grown-ups* who owned BMWs.

Michelle's room was on the fourth floor of a dorm, in a cozy attic with sloped ceilings. One of her roommates was a white girl named Catherine. She was from New Orleans, in the Deep South. She seemed nice and friendly.

But after a few months, Catherine moved to a different dorm. Years later Michelle found out why. Catherine's mother had been shocked to learn that her daughter had a black roommate. She demanded that her daughter's room be changed. The woman told officials at Princeton, "We weren't used to living with black people."

Catherine wasn't the only white student at Princeton who hadn't known African Americans before college. Although the white students were not openly racist, they tended to leave minorities out of their social life.

One example was the "eating clubs" at Princeton, which were like fraternities. Each club had its own beautiful building, with a fancy dining hall. The clubs held parties and dances, too.

Like fraternities, students could only join a club if they were invited. But in 1981, when Michelle was at Princeton, all the eating clubs were almost completely white.

Imagine how hurt Michelle must have felt, knowing that she and her friends weren't asked to join any clubs because of the color of their skin.

Michelle and her friends gathered in the Third World Center instead. They could play music there, and eat and talk. It became their social club.

Still, Michelle thought that Princeton should try harder to bring black and white students together. In her last year in college, Michelle wrote a paper about how it felt to be black at Princeton. It had made her far more aware of her "blackness" than ever before. Sometimes she felt like a visitor on campus.

In 1985, Michelle graduated from Princeton with honors. That was proof that she had been a better student than most.

Now what? Michelle wasn't sure what to do next. But she knew she wanted to help people. Was law school the answer?

Having done so well at Princeton, Michelle was ready to aim even higher. Many people thought Harvard University had the best law school—so of course that's where Michelle wanted to go.

And with her determination, of course she got in!

Chapter 3
Meeting Barack

In the fall of 1985, Michelle entered Harvard Law School. At first, she wasn't sure she liked it. Maybe law school had been a mistake. What mattered most to Michelle was helping people—especially people who couldn't help themselves. So in her spare time, she worked in an office where Harvard Law students gave advice to people who couldn't afford lawyers.

HARVARD LAW SCHOOL

In the summer, Michelle worked at a law firm back home in Chicago. The law firm was called Sidley Austin. Michelle's summer job was sort of like a tryout. If she did well, she might be hired for a full-time job after she graduated.

Michelle did very well at Sidley. So when she graduated from law school in 1988, Sidley Austin offered her a good job, with a high salary.

Now at age twenty-four, she was making a lot

more money than her father! She needed a good salary to pay off her hefty student loans from Princeton and Harvard.

After seven years away, Michelle was so happy to be back in the city she loved.

But what about the work itself? Michelle did legal work for a dinosaur—a famous purple dinosaur named Barney! Michelle's job was to work on contracts for Barney toys, books, and games.

The other lawyers at Sidley thought Michelle was lucky. Her assignment was fun. But Michelle didn't love the work. She wished she could do something to help poor people, and maybe even change the world.

One day, a new person came to work at Sidley. He was a Harvard Law student, like Michelle had been, and this was his summer job. Michelle was assigned to be his mentor. She would teach him about the law firm.

The summer associate was Barack Obama.

Michelle's friends at Sidley had seen a picture of Barack. He was tall and had a great smile. He was supposed to be brilliant. Everyone thought Michelle Robinson and Barack Obama would make a good couple.

Everyone except Michelle, that is. How would it look if she dated a guy when she was supposed to be teaching him about work?

Michelle was perfectly friendly to Barack. She went out to lunch with him—but it was a business lunch, not a date.

She talked to him at office parties and gave him a ride home sometimes. She even tried to set him up with her friends. But Barack didn't want to date her friends. He wanted to date Michelle. He kept asking her out. Finally, he wore her down.

For their first real date, they went to the movies.

After that, they spent a lot of time together. One day Barack took her to a church basement. He was there to speak at a community meeting. Michelle saw how special he was. Barack was sincere about wanting to help people. She started to fall in love with him right then and there.

Michelle grew to like Barack so much that she brought him home to meet her family! That was a big deal for Michelle. She didn't do it too often.

Craig felt sorry for Barack

the first time they met. So did her parents. They knew Michelle was very picky. She usually only dated guys for a short time. If they did one thing wrong she "fired them," according to Craig. But a month later, Michelle asked Craig to do her a favor. She wanted Craig to play basketball with Barack—and Craig knew why.

Craig and his dad believed that you could tell a lot about a person from the way he played basketball. Did he hog the ball? Was he afraid to shoot and miss? Did he show off on the court? Or lie about being fouled? Craig set up a game at a local school with a lot of his friends. They were all excellent players like Craig.

The game was tough and competitive. But Barack played well. He wanted to win, but he didn't argue about every little thing in the game.

"He was confident without being cocky," Craig said. After the game, he told Michelle that Barack was a good guy.

Great! Michelle thought. There was only one problem. Barack had to go back to Harvard Law at the end of the summer. For the next two years, Michelle and Barack saw each other only occasionally. Barack came to Chicago for the summer. Michelle went with him to Hawaii at Christmas, to visit his family. She and Barack wrote letters and talked on the phone.

Then something terrible happened. Michelle's

father suddenly died after an operation. No one had expected it.

Michelle was devastated. Her father had meant everything to her. Barack flew to Chicago for the funeral. He was at Michelle's side for the saddest period in her life. But would he always be there?

Michelle was beginning to wonder. Barack said it wasn't important to be married. He didn't want to promise anything. All that mattered was their love for each other.

Then one night he took Michelle out to dinner. He had finished school. He was a lawyer now! They went to a fancy restaurant to celebrate.

At the dinner, they started talking about marriage again. Michelle was getting frustrated, because Barack was saying the same old thing: Marriage wasn't important. Then a waiter brought out a special dessert. There, on the plate, was a box with an engagement ring in it. Barack had been planning to propose all along!

ELEANOR ROOSEVELT
OCTOBER 11, 1884–NOVEMBER 7, 1962

ELEANOR ROOSEVELT'S UNCLE WAS TEDDY ROOSEVELT. HE WAS PRESIDENT OF THE UNITED STATES FROM 1901-1909, WHEN SHE WAS A TEENAGER.

THEN ONE DAY ELEANOR RAN INTO ANOTHER ROOSEVELT ON A TRAIN. IT WAS FRANKLIN D. ROOSEVELT. HE WAS A DISTANT COUSIN. THEY FELL IN LOVE AND GOT MARRIED. FRANKLIN D. ROOSEVELT WAS FIRST ELECTED PRESIDENT IN 1932. HE BECAME ONE OF THE MOST FAMOUS AND BELOVED PRESIDENTS IN US HISTORY. HE WAS KNOWN AS FDR. HE LED THE COUNTRY THROUGH THE GREAT DEPRESSION AND WORLD WAR II.

BUT ELEANOR WAS JUST AS BELOVED AS FIRST LADY. SHE WAS ONE OF THE MOST OUTSPOKEN WOMEN OF HER TIME, AND ONE OF THE MOST FAMOUS WOMEN IN THE WORLD. SHE GAVE SPEECHES ALL OVER THE COUNTRY. SHE SPOKE OUT IN FAVOR OF CIVIL RIGHTS—THE RIGHTS THAT ALL PEOPLE OF EVERY RACE ARE SUPPOSED TO HAVE, TO BE TREATED EQUALLY AND FAIRLY.

BECAUSE POLIO HAD MADE FDR UNABLE TO WALK, ELEANOR TRAVELED CONSTANTLY. SHE WAS HER HUSBAND'S EYES AND EARS. SHE HELD MORE

THAN THREE HUNDRED PRESS CONFERENCES
WHILE FDR WAS PRESIDENT. SHE ALSO WROTE A
NEWSPAPER COLUMN ABOUT HER WORK AND LIFE.
IT WAS PUBLISHED SIX DAYS A WEEK FOR MORE
THAN TWENTY-FIVE YEARS!

WHEN FDR LEFT THE WHITE HOUSE, MANY
PEOPLE SAID ELEANOR SHOULD RUN FOR OFFICE.
SHE CHOSE NOT TO. IF SHE HAD, SHE MIGHT HAVE
BECOME THE FIRST WOMAN PRESIDENT.

Chapter 4
Making Choices

Besides marriage, Michelle was also thinking about her career. Her work paid well, but she didn't love it. Maybe Michelle would be happier in a new job—doing work for poor people in her own community. That was what Barack planned to do.

Michelle met with a woman named Valerie Jarrett. Valerie worked for the mayor of Chicago. She offered Michelle a job immediately.

But Michelle wanted time to think. She was being picky—as always. Did she want to work

VALERIE JARRETT

for a politician? There weren't many she admired. Barack felt the same about politicians—but not about politics. He thought politics—passing good laws—was a way to make a real difference in people's lives. He encouraged Michelle to take the job, and she did.

On October 3, 1992, Michelle and Barack got married. Michelle's friend Santita Jackson sang at the wedding.

For a short time the couple lived with Michelle's mother—in the same small apartment where Michelle had grown up. But pretty soon they got their own apartment in a nice neighborhood called Hyde Park.

Michelle's new job paid less, so the Obamas didn't have much money. And they both still had big student loans to pay off. Barack was working two jobs. He taught at the University of Chicago Law School. He also did legal work for people in poor neighborhoods. What he most wanted to do, however, was run for political office.

Politics. Michelle wasn't thrilled with the idea. Running for office was expensive. Could they afford it and still afford to have children? What about all the money they owed? And what about all the time it would take? Barack wanted to be elected to the state government in Springfield, the capital of Illinois. It was two hundred miles away! Barack would have to spend a lot of time there.

Still, Michelle wanted her husband to achieve his dreams. She agreed that he should run, even though it would be hard on their marriage. In 1996, Barack Obama ran for the Illinois State Senate—and won. Now he would represent the part of Chicago where they lived. At the time, Michelle had no idea that this was just the beginning of Barack's political career. She certainly didn't know it would lead to the White House!

VISION · INTEGRITY · COMMITMENT

ELECT

BARACK OBAMA

For State Senate

DEMOCRAT

DOLLEY MADISON
MAY 20, 1768–JULY 12, 1849

DOLLEY PAYNE TODD MARRIED JAMES MADISON WHEN SHE WAS TWENTY-FIVE YEARS OLD. SHE WAS ALREADY A WIDOW. HER FIRST HUSBAND HAD DIED FROM YELLOW FEVER. SO HAD HER YOUNGEST SON.

BEFORE MADISON BECAME PRESIDENT, DOLLEY OFTEN SERVED AS A KIND OF FIRST LADY FOR THOMAS JEFFERSON. THAT WAS BECAUSE HE HAD NO WIFE! SHE HOSTED WONDERFUL PARTIES FOR HIM IN THE WHITE HOUSE. AFTER JEFFERSON LEFT OFFICE, MADISON WAS ELECTED PRESIDENT. DOLLEY WAS THE REAL FIRST LADY NOW. AT HER HUSBAND'S SECOND INAUGURATION, SHE SERVED A NEW TREAT. STRAWBERRY ICE CREAM!

IN 1812, THE UNITED STATES WAS AT WAR AGAIN WITH ENGLAND. THE BRITISH STORMED INTO WASHINGTON TO SET THE WHITE HOUSE ON FIRE! DOLLEY MADISON WAS INSIDE. SHE REFUSED TO LEAVE UNTIL SHE HELPED SAVE AN IMPORTANT PAINTING OF GEORGE WASHINGTON.

Chapter 5
A New Family

With Barack often in Springfield, Michelle tried to find satisfaction in her work. For almost four years, she worked as the director of a group that got young people involved in community work. Then Michelle took a job at the University of Chicago. There she found ways for college students to become involved with neighborhood projects for the poor.

At the same time, Michelle was ready to start another kind of project. A family!

But what would family life be like for two hardworking parents?

Michelle and Barack had had very different childhoods. Barack said that Michelle's family reminded him of a TV show from the 1950s

called *Leave It to Beaver*. On the show, the family seemed perfect.

Barack's childhood hadn't been as happy. He had been born in Hawaii. His parents separated when Barack was only two years old. His father, who was from Kenya, returned to Africa.

Later his mother got married to a man from

Indonesia. She took Barack to live there when he was six years old. Eventually, Barack returned to Hawaii and lived with his grandparents. He only saw his own father once more.

It is easy to see why Barack's idea of family wasn't the same as Michelle's.

Their first child, Malia, was born on the Fourth of July in 1998.

Three years later, Natasha was born. They called her Sasha for short.

Michelle wanted to raise her children the way she had been brought up. However, the Obamas' life as new parents was very different from Michelle's parents'. Michelle was working full time, and Barack was away a lot.

It was very tough for Michelle, raising two small children often by herself.

Michelle felt angry a lot of the time, and Barack knew it.

But Barack and Michelle were crazy about their girls. When Barack was home, the family had fun together. Barack also did chores around the house—because Michelle insisted!

Michelle's mother, Marian, was able to help out a great deal with Malia and Sasha. As they

got older, she picked them up at school. She took them to the playground. She took Malia to dance lessons and soccer games. She cooked the same meals she had made when Michelle was little.

Still, day-to-day life was hard. Michelle was unhappy.

Barack also continued to have bigger dreams.

In 2000, Barack ran to become a congressman in the US House of

Representatives. It was a tough election, and he lost. Michelle hoped he might quit politics after that. And after such a loss, many people would have quit. But not Barack Obama. He simply decided he was never going to lose again.

JACQUELINE BOUVIER KENNEDY
JULY 28, 1929–MAY 19, 1994

JOHN F. KENNEDY WAS ELECTED PRESIDENT IN 1960. HE WAS CALLED JACK, OR JFK. JACQUELINE WAS ONLY THIRTY-ONE YEARS OLD— ONE OF THE YOUNGEST FIRST LADIES. SHE WAS BEAUTIFUL AND GLAMOROUS. HER CLOTHES WERE ALL MADE BY FRENCH DESIGNERS. TO MANY PEOPLE, IT SEEMED LIKE THE KENNEDYS WERE ALMOST ROYALTY. (NEWSPAPERS AND MAGAZINES CALLED THEM JACK AND JACKIE, BUT SHE ALWAYS CALLED HERSELF JACQUELINE.)

THE WHITE HOUSE WAS IN VERY RUN-DOWN SHAPE WHEN THE KENNEDYS MOVED IN. JACKIE REDECORATED AND TURNED IT INTO A PLACE THAT AMERICANS COULD BE PROUD OF.

WHEN THE REFURNISHING WAS DONE, JACKIE BROUGHT IN TELEVISION CAMERAS. SHE GAVE A TOUR OF THE WHITE HOUSE. MILLIONS OF PEOPLE WATCHED IT. ON TV, HER VOICE WAS SURPRISINGLY SOFT AND SHY.

JOHN KENNEDY'S PRESIDENCY WAS CUT SHORT WHEN HE WAS SHOT AND KILLED IN DALLAS, TEXAS, IN NOVEMBER OF 1963.

THE WHOLE NATION WAS IN SHOCK AND GRIEF. AT THE FUNERAL, SHE HELD HER TWO CHILDREN

BESIDE HER. SHE WORE A BLACK VEIL OVER HER FACE AND LOOKED VERY BRAVE. EVEN IN TRAGEDY, JACKIE KENNEDY BEHAVED LIKE A QUEEN.

SHE IS REMEMBERED FOR BEING A VERY PRIVATE PERSON WHO KEPT HER CHILDREN OUT OF THE PUBLIC EYE. LIKE MICHELLE OBAMA, SHE WANTED TO MAKE SURE HER CHILDREN WOULD GROW UP TO HAVE NORMAL, HAPPY LIVES.

Chapter 6
Politics

In 2003, Barack Obama decided to aim for an even higher public office. He was going to run for the US Senate. Michelle wasn't sure about Barack's decision. If Barack became a senator, it could change a lot of things for their family. They would either have to move to Washington, DC,

or live apart a lot of the time. Michelle didn't want to move. Her job at the University of Chicago was important to her. And her salary was important to the family.

Also, home for Sasha and Malia was in Chicago. Michelle didn't want their lives to change. So if Barack won the election, he would go to Washington alone. The Obamas would need two houses. Barack would have even less time to spend with Michelle and the girls.

Michelle decided to go along with Barack's plan. She knew how important it was to African Americans everywhere. There had only been four black senators in Congress—ever. Besides, Barack promised that if he lost, he would quit politics forever. Sometimes Michelle even joked that she hoped he'd lose!

It didn't seem like Barack would lose, though. By the spring of 2004, Barack was capturing the attention of voters all across Illinois. Everyone wanted to know: Who was this new guy who made such exciting speeches?

A few months later, Barack was invited to give an important speech at the Democratic National Convention. The convention was a big meeting held every four years to choose a candidate for president. Usually only well-known politicians spoke at the convention. Barack Obama wasn't even a member of Congress yet! It was a big honor to be chosen.

Michelle understood the importance of the speech. Barack would be seen on TV by millions of Americans. If he did a good job, it would help him get elected to the US Senate in the fall.

Barack stood backstage, waiting to go on. Michelle could tell Barack was nervous. Everyone was! Michelle's brother, Craig, was so nervous he was sweating. Barack's staff were worried about what tie Barack should wear. At the last minute, they had him switch ties with one of the staff.

To calm Barack down, Michelle decided to tease him a little bit. She told him that he'd better not mess up!

He didn't.

Barack gave a speech so exciting, it made people cry. He said that there wasn't a white America and a black America. There was just the United States of America. Only in America could a skinny black kid with a funny name believe that America had a place for him, too.

At the end, the audience jumped to its feet. People were cheering and shouting. Barack Obama was a star. Michelle felt so proud!

The next day, millions of people were talking about this new young politician. People all over America—not just in Chicago—were fascinated

by him. In the fall, Barack won the election. He was now a US senator from the state of Illinois.

Michelle, Malia, and Sasha all went to Washington with him in January. They wanted to be there to see Barack sworn in as a senator. Michelle smiled a huge smile in the photograph taken that day. Earlier that day, Malia had asked a question: "Daddy, are you going to be president?" Barack didn't answer. He knew a lot of reporters were listening. He wasn't going to share his hopes with the world. However, in his heart, he must have known right then what his biggest dream of all was.

MARY TODD LINCOLN
DECEMBER 13, 1818–JULY 16, 1882

LIKE MICHELLE OBAMA, MARY TODD LINCOLN OFTEN FOUND HERSELF ALONE IN ILLINOIS WITH HER CHILDREN. SHE STAYED HOME WHILE HER HUSBAND, ABRAHAM LINCOLN, WAS A CONGRESSMAN IN WASHINGTON. SADLY, SHE WAS NOT A STRONG PERSON IN THE WAY MICHELLE OBAMA IS.

MARY SUFFERED FROM BAD HEADACHES. SHE WAS SAD AND DEPRESSED MUCH OF THE TIME.

TWO OF HER SONS DIED IN CHILDHOOD. IT BROKE HER HEART AND SENT HER INTO VERY DARK MOODS.

PRESIDENT LINCOLN LED THE COUNTRY DURING THE CIVIL WAR. MARY WAS A HELP TO HIM— SHE STOOD UP AGAINST SLAVERY. SHE VISITED WOUNDED UNION SOLDIERS IN THE HOSPITAL. BUT SHE'D LOSE HER TEMPER IN FRONT OF IMPORTANT PEOPLE. HER BAD MOODS WERE HARD TO TAKE.

MARY WAS WITH HER HUSBAND AT THE THE-ATER THE NIGHT HE WAS SHOT IN APRIL 1865. SHE WAS SO OVERCOME WITH GRIEF, SHE COULDN'T GO TO HIS FUNERAL. BEFORE SHE LEFT THE WHITE HOUSE, SHE GAVE ABE LINCOLN'S BEST WALKING STICK TO FREDERICK DOUGLASS, A FORMER SLAVE.

Chapter 7
Race for the White House

Now that Barack was in Washington as a senator, Michelle was even lonelier. But she decided not to be upset all the time. Instead, she figured out how to make things work. She got up early each day so she could go to the gym and work out.

She hired more babysitters. She asked her mother to help out more often with the girls.

Life was easier for another reason, too. The Obamas no longer had to worry about money. Many years before, Barack had written a book, *Dreams from My Father*. It was about his childhood and growing up. After his stirring speech at the 2004 convention, the book became a best seller.

The Obamas were able to buy a six-bedroom house.

Michelle felt much more secure about their future. She was proud of Barack, too. He was doing important work in Congress. He helped pass a law to reduce the number of nuclear weapons in Europe and Russia. He spoke out against the war in Iraq. He also talked about helping the victims of Hurricane Katrina.

So Michelle wasn't surprised when Barack told her that he wanted to run for president. And she didn't object. She simply asked a lot of questions: Could he really win? Where would the girls go to school? How would it change their lives? Would they be safe? Would the girls have any privacy?

And could Barack beat Hillary Clinton, the senator from New York who wanted to be the next Democratic candidate for president?

Barack had good answers for all of her questions. He believed he could win the nomination and the election. They could keep the girls safe and raise them the way they both wanted to. However, Barack left the final decision on this big step to Michelle. If she didn't agree, he wouldn't run.

Michelle mulled it over. She knew some things would be hard. But she also realized how important this was, not just to Barack. It would be a turning point for the whole country, to have the first African American president. As the first black First Lady, Michelle would make history, too.

Finally Michelle said yes—yes, Barack should run for president. But she asked him to promise two things. Barack had to quit smoking.

And he had to promise that Malia and Sasha could get a puppy after the election—whether Barack won or lost.

Barack announced his candidacy to the world in February 2007. From that point on, he and Michelle were busy day and night. Michelle cut back on her job. She only worked a few hours a week. That way she'd have time to help out with the campaign.

To keep herself healthy, she worked out three times a week.

At the same time, she tried to keep their family life stable. She tried to have dinner with the girls every night.

Voters, however, wanted to meet her, to find out what she was like. People were fascinated with her as well as her husband. This meant traveling to many different states.

So Michelle made some rules for herself. She would only leave Chicago one day a week. She would be home for Malia and Sasha's soccer games, parent conferences, and dance recitals.

She tried to be home every night before the girls went to bed. Michelle also bought two laptop computers. That way, she and Barack could video chat with their daughters whenever they were away. And as always Marian Robinson helped take care of the children.

It was tiring, but Michelle didn't mind, because her daughters were happy. "The girls—they just think Mommy was at work," Michelle said. "They don't know I was in New Hampshire."

Michelle was a very honest, open person. She joked a lot on the campaign trail and didn't mince words. Sometimes she said things that got her in trouble.

Once, she told a crowd that Barack's run for the presidency made her really proud of her country "for the first time in my adult life."

Her comment caused
an uproar. Michelle
probably meant that
Barack's campaign
made her feel *more*
proud than ever before.
But that's not what she
said. Her words made
it sound like she wasn't
proud of America until
now. The quote was all
over the news.

After that, Michelle was more careful about
what she said. But she was still honest and open.

People loved her,
and many shared her
values. She talked a lot
about working hard,
doing your best, and
putting family first.

In August, a few months before the election, *People* magazine wrote an article about the family. It included the Obama family's House Rules.

Rule #1 was: No whining, arguing, or annoying teasing.

Rule #2: Make the bed. "Doesn't have to look good—just throw the sheet over it."

They also had a rule about Christmas, which the family often spent in Hawaii. Michelle and

Barack didn't give their daughters any presents. Michelle thought Santa brought enough presents for the kids. She didn't want her daughters to be spoiled.

In November 2008, Barack Obama was elected president. Michelle became a First Lady, who looked nothing like the First Ladies who had come before her. For the first time in history, there was a young, beautiful, talented black family living in the White House. It was an exciting and inspiring time in America.

BETTY FORD
APRIL 8, 1918–JULY 8, 2011

AS A TEENAGER, ELIZABETH ANN "BETTY" BLOOMER LOVED TO DANCE. SHE MODELED CLOTHES WHEN SHE WAS FOURTEEN. THEN SHE STUDIED DANCE WITH THE FAMOUS CHOREOGRAPHER MARTHA GRAHAM. SHE EVEN PERFORMED AS A DANCER AT CARNEGIE HALL!

BETTY MARRIED TWICE. HER FIRST HUSBAND WAS WILLIAM WARREN. HE DRANK TOO MUCH, SO BETTY DIVORCED HIM. HER SECOND HUSBAND WAS GERALD FORD. HE BECAME VICE PRESIDENT UNDER RICHARD NIXON. THEN HE BECAME PRESIDENT WHEN NIXON RESIGNED IN DISGRACE.

IN THE WHITE HOUSE, BETTY FORD WAS VERY OUTSPOKEN. SHE TALKED OPENLY ABOUT EVERYTHING—INCLUDING HER OWN BREAST CANCER. UNTIL THEN, PEOPLE HADN'T TALKED IN PUBLIC ABOUT THAT DISEASE. SHE ALSO SPOKE OUT IN FAVOR OF WOMEN'S RIGHTS. SHE WORKED HARD TO GET THE EQUAL RIGHTS AMENDMENT PASSED.

AFTER SHE LEFT THE WHITE HOUSE, BETTY DID SOMETHING ELSE BRAVE. SHE ADMITTED THAT SHE DRANK TOO MUCH HERSELF! SHE TOLD THE WORLD ABOUT HER PROBLEMS WITH ALCOHOL AND PILLS. THEN SHE STARTED A CLINIC TO HELP PEOPLE WITH ADDICTION. IT WAS CALLED THE BETTY FORD CENTER.

IN 1991, PRESIDENT GEORGE W. BUSH GAVE BETTY FORD AN AWARD. IT WAS THE PRESIDENTIAL MEDAL OF FREEDOM—THE HIGHEST CIVILIAN HONOR THAT THE US GOVERNMENT GIVES.

Chapter 8
First Lady

On January 20, 2009, the Obamas moved into the White House.

It was the day of the inauguration—the big ceremony to swear in the new president.

According to the Constitution, the president would be sworn in at exactly noon. Barack stood on the steps of

LINCOLN BIBLE

the Capitol. Michelle smiled as she held a famous Bible in her hands. It was Abraham Lincoln's Bible.

Millions of people watched the ceremony on television. They knew they were witnessing an important moment in history.

Malia and Sasha were there, too. At seven, Sasha was so little, she had to stand on a wooden box to see the swearing in!

The inauguration was more than a one-day event. It was like a huge party. There was an amazing concert a few days before. The biggest pop stars in America performed on the steps of the Lincoln Memorial.

Barack also held a King Day of Service, named for Martin Luther King Jr. Barack, Michelle, Malia, and Sasha all did volunteer work that day to help soldiers in Iraq.

After the inauguration, there were parades, luncheons, and celebrations. That night, there was a series of fancy balls for the new president. Everyone waited to see what Michelle would wear. Her beautiful long white gown was stunning.

Michelle and Barack danced at ten balls that night.

For their first dance, the pop star Beyoncé sang a romantic song called "At Last." The song was about two people in love finally being together. One of the lyrics said: "My lonely days are over."

For Michelle, it was especially true. Her lonely days *were* over. Now, for the first time in many years, the family would be living together full-time. Barack's office would be in the same place where he lived—the White House. He would be able to walk upstairs at six thirty every night and eat dinner with Michelle and the girls.

A few hours after the inauguration, Michelle, Barack, and the girls moved into the White House.

When they arrived, it looked like they already lived there! Malia's clothes were hung in her closet. Sasha's toys were arranged on her dresser. Their posters of the Jonas Brothers were already up on the walls!

How could it happen so fast? The White House staff was very organized. They unpacked everything in six hours. They knew where to put everything because they had taken pictures in the Obama family's Chicago home.

Michelle Obama made some rules on the first day. She told the staff that Malia and Sasha still had to do chores. They had to make their beds themselves and pick up their toys. She wanted them to have as normal a life as possible.

Of course the White House wasn't a normal house. There was a bowling alley, a swimming

pool, and a movie theater inside! There were three
elevators and thirty-five bathrooms. On the top
floor, there was a game room with a pool table.

Part of the White House was used for special

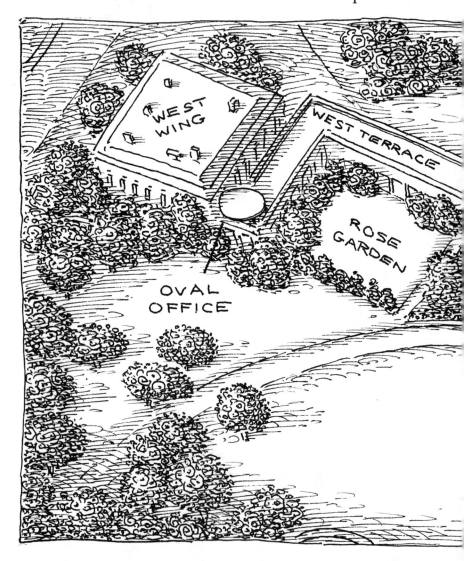

events—concerts, balls, and formal dinners. But
the president's family didn't live in those rooms.
They lived upstairs on the second and third floors,
in rooms that were cozier and more private.

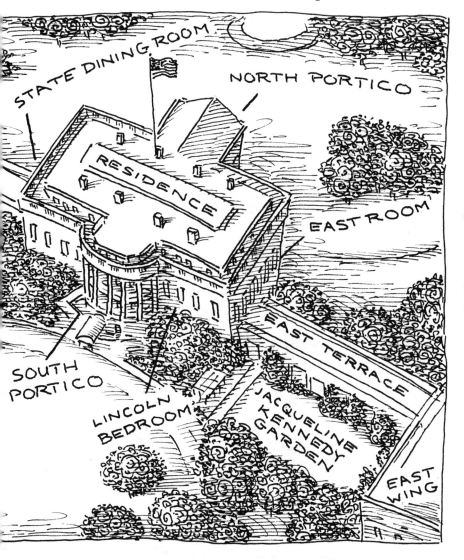

Michelle's job as First Lady was to act as hostess for important events. She was in charge of formal dinners when presidents, kings, and queens came to visit. She traveled to foreign countries to represent America when Barack couldn't go.

Living in the White House wasn't always fun. The Obamas couldn't go anywhere without the Secret Service to protect them.

On Halloween, Sasha and Malia tried to
go trick-or-treating in a regular neighborhood.
But people mobbed the girls and started taking
pictures. The girls had to go home.

That was one thing Michelle was very strict
about. She had made a rule that the press
couldn't take pictures of Malia and Sasha without
permission. The press respected the rule and gave
the girls plenty of privacy.

Another time, Barack took Michelle to New York City. He had promised her a date—dinner and a Broadway show. They flew on Air Force One. Of course the Secret Service had to come along. They didn't have much privacy. Then reporters criticized the president for spending taxpayers' money for a night out in New York!

The Secret Service had code names for each family member. The president's code name was

THE PRESIDENT'S OVAL OFFICE

AIR FORCE ONE BOEING VC-25A

Renegade. Michelle's was Renaissance. Malia's was Radiance. Sasha's was Rosebud. (By tradition, the code names for a president's family all have the same first letter.)

Barack Obama was the commander in chief, but Michelle called herself the "mom in chief." She said being a good parent was her most important job. To help out, Michelle's mother moved into

the White House, too. Marian Robinson was "the First Grandma." She took the girls to school every day at Sidwell Friends, a private school, and took care of them whenever Michelle was away.

Barack kept his promises to Michelle. He quit smoking, although it took him a few years to really stop. They also got a puppy for Malia and Sasha. The fuzzy black-and-white dog was a Portuguese water dog. They named him Bo.

Michelle became an incredibly popular
First Lady. From the inauguration on, she was
known as a fashion star. Some clothes were from
expensive, fancy designers. Some were from
popular stores like Target or J. Crew. But whatever
she wore, she always looked fabulous.

As always, Michelle wanted to make a
difference in people's lives. She started a program

to help kids stay healthy. First, she planted a vegetable garden at the White House. She invited kids from a local school to help. The White House chefs used the vegetables in meals for the family. Michelle hoped that kids all over America would eat more healthy foods.

In 2010, Michelle started a program called "Let's Move." Getting exercise was just as important as eating right. That's why she had been teaching kids to hula-hoop on the White House lawn. She suggested that schools stay open in the evenings, so that families could come play basketball. Towns could create more bike lanes and walking paths. Michelle hoped more kids would walk to school.

She also wanted to help military families. Michelle started a program called "Joining Forces." Michelle believed that while a mother or father was fighting a war overseas, the rest of the family was also serving the country. These families often had to pick up and move from one military base to another. Often soldiers were stationed far away. This was hard on everyone in the family. Michelle wanted Americans to show appreciation for the sacrifices made by military families.

Michelle was so popular that she helped her husband get elected to a second term as president. In September 2012, she gave a brilliant, moving speech at the Democratic convention in Charlotte, North Carolina. She talked about the things she and Barack believed in. They believed you should work hard for what you want in life. They believed you should always keep your word and do what you say you're going to do. They believed you should treat people with dignity and respect, even if you don't know them, and even if you don't agree with them.

Like Barack's speech in 2004, her speech was so good that it made people cry, cheer, and leap to their feet. The photos taken of Michelle that night showed her smiling and beautiful. It made voters want to believe in Barack when his confident, smart, good-hearted wife believed in him so strongly.

Sasha, Malia, and Barack watched Michelle on

TV as she gave the speech. Malia was a teenager starting high school. Pretty soon she'd be learning how to drive! Sasha was eleven. They weren't little girls now. They were growing up.

In November, Barack Obama was elected for
a second term as president. A photo of Michelle
and Barack hugging that night was tweeted by

the White House. It became the most retweeted photo in history.

On January 21, 2013, Barack Obama was

sworn in for a second term before a massive crowd. The ceremony fell on the same day that Martin Luther King Jr.'s birthday was celebrated. When Barack Obama took the oath of office, he placed his hands on both Abraham Lincoln's Bible and a Bible that had belonged to Reverend King.

This time the White House staff did not have to rush to move furniture into the White House. Michelle Obama and her family were happy and comfortable there now. She looked forward to another four years as First Lady, speaking out for good causes, and raising her daughters in Washington. After all, the family was together. Family—that's what had always been most important to Michelle Obama.

TIMELINE OF
MICHELLE OBAMA'S LIFE

1964 —— Michelle LaVaughn Robinson is born in Chicago, Illinois

1977 —— Michelle attends Whitney M. Young Magnet High School, Chicago's first magnet high school for gifted children

1981 —— Michelle arrives at Princeton University

1985 —— Michelle graduates from Princeton with honors
Michelle enters Harvard Law School

1988 —— Michelle graduates from law school
Michelle becomes an associate attorney of the law firm Sidley Austin, focusing on marketing and intellectual property

1992 —— Michelle marries Barack Obama

1996 —— Barack is elected to the Illinois State Senate

1998 —— Daughter Malia is born

2001 —— Daughter Sasha is born

2008 —— Barack is elected the forty-fourth president of the United States

2009 —— The Obamas move into the White House
Michelle encourages healthy eating for US kids and grows a vegetable garden at the White House

2010 —— Michelle starts the program Let's Move

2012 —— Michelle gives a moving speech at the Democratic convention in Charlotte, North Carolina
Barack is reelected to serve a second term as president

TIMELINE OF
THE WORLD

Four young African American men protest segregation by sitting at the whites-only lunch counter at a Woolworth's in Greensboro, North Carolina	1960
Martin Luther King Jr. makes his famous "I Have a Dream" speech at the March on Washington for Jobs and Freedom	1963
Congress passes the Civil Rights Act of 1964, which bans racial discrimination in public places	1964
National Organization for Women (NOW) is founded	1966
Thurgood Marshall becomes the first African American US Supreme Court justice	1967
Martin Luther King Jr. is assassinated	1968
President Richard Nixon resigns	1974
Margaret Thatcher becomes the first woman prime minister of Great Britain	1979
Sandra Day O'Connor becomes the first woman appointed to the US Supreme Court	1981
Sally Ride becomes the first American woman to go into space	1983
The Berlin Wall falls	1989
On September 11, terrorists attack the Twin Towers in New York City and the Pentagon in Washington, DC	2001
The Iraq War begins	2003
Osama bin Laden, the man behind the September 11, 2001, attacks, is killed The Iraq War ends	2011
Park Geun-hye is the first woman to be elected president of South Korea	2012

BIBLIOGRAPHY

*Brophy, David Bergen. **Michelle Obama: Meet the First Lady.** New York: Collins, 2009.

*Colbert, David. **Michelle Obama: An American Story.** Boston: Houghton Mifflin, 2009.

Kantor, Jodi. **The Obamas.** New York: Little Brown, 2012.

Mundy, Liza. **Michelle: A Biography.** New York: Simon & Schuster, 2008.

Murray, Shailagh. **"A Family Tree Rooted in American Soil."** *Washington Post*, October 2, 2008.

Rogak, Lisa, editor. **Michelle Obama: In Her Own Words.** New York: Public Affairs, 2009.

Westfall, Sandra Sobieraj. **"The Obamas Get Personal."** *People*, August 4, 2008.

* Books for young readers